Here It Goes

Alex Hanna

ISBN: 0-9990694-0-3
ISBN-13: 978-0-9990694-0-0

DEDICATION

This is dedicated to anyone who has struggled to give their emotions a voice.

CONTENTS

ACKNOWLEDGMENTS

I would like to thank my loving wife, who has supported me through every step of the way, even when fighting against the most insurmountable enemies. And I would like to acknowledge my sister, who continues to share love, strength, and poetry with me to this day.

1 LIGHT

Here It Goes

Life is short—
Too short.
Don't shut the world out;
Don't live with doubt.

Each life around you—
All around you—
Carries a unique story
Of losses and of glory.

And I know
That I know:
Vulnerability I must expose,
Insecurity I must dispose.
So, here it goes...

Golden Sun

The golden sun whispers a sleepy "hello"
as she slips from underneath the cozy sheets.
Her rested eyes yawn as the still night
draws to a close.

One by one, her luminous legs stretch down.
Her toes delicately kiss the ground.
With arms spread wide, reaching
to the ends of the Earth
with a welcoming embrace.

She greets today as she does every other:
ardently hopeful. She shines,
offering forgiveness for all of yesterdays
clouded indiscretions.

She looks down on you and gently smiles—
the most honest will, bestowed.
Your day graced with sustaining light:
her gift to you, each and every day.

I Forgive Myself

I forgive myself
for each past sin:
For every transgression,
for my demons within.

I will learn to accept
me for who I am:
For where I've been,
for my failures to stand.

I will allow my emotions
to finally flow through.
Unbroken by rocks,
my fears subdued.

The day will come
when I will stand tall;
Knowing full-well
I will continue to fall.

But each time I fall,
I vow to rise again.
And until that day comes,
forgiveness I shall extend.

Let Go of My Hand

Let go of my hand
It's ok
I need to know if I can stand

I may fall, but
It's ok
I refuse to crawl

You may see the scrapes that cover my knees
It's ok
Let go of my hand...please

I asked you to hold me tight
It's ok
I need to know I tried to fight

You've carried my burdens, dragged me along
It's ok
But you've put yourself second for far too long

When my knees start to bleed
It's ok
No more can you ignore your needs

The westerly winds will blow
It's ok
My strength will come from the example you shone

The clouds will cover the blue
It's ok
I'm here to support you

And when the storm seems too strong to weather
It's ok

We'll make it through together

So let go of my hand
It's ok
Side-by-side
Forever
We will stand.

Breathe in the Cool

I breathe in the cool, calming warmth you radiate.
I expel the burning insecurities plaguing my mind—
Renewing my soul with your gift of purity,
Ridding my body of all that burdens my most inner peace.

I allow the negative energy
to pass through
my rumbling lips,
shedding the discomfort
which has nestled into my every thought.

Leave me—wretched nightmares!
For I welcome love and warmth
to replace your horrid, putrid ways.
Bless those who have gifted their light—
When darkness all but claimed victory.

Home

Home—
Where the humming of the radiator
meets the whistle of silence.

The creaking of the neighbor's staircase
joins in harmony with the pitter-patter
of the cat's sneaky footsteps on the hardwood floor.
A passing car completes the chord.

Home—
Where the breath from my lungs
makes love with the beat of your heart.

Only this could be Home.

Supple Salt

Close, so close,
I feel your every breath.
Close, so close,
Each hair on my neck
stretches, sweats, drips
with desire, longing to taste
the supple salt of temptation
which lingers on your lips.

Midnight Musings

As the moon takes rise
over dreary skies,
your weary eyes
slowly close.

And when the moon crests,
you deeply rest.
Dreams beget
sweet prose.

And now the moon sleeps,
while her musings repeat.
My awakened soul piqued:
Romantic dreams she stows.

As the dawn takes rise,
over once-dreary skies,
your cloudless eyes
smile atop weary woes.

Teetering, Teetering

Teetering, teetering, on the edge of despair.
On this precipice I stand so high.
Breathing, breathing, this heavenly air,
So drunk on this bliss I could fly.

Flying, flying, weightless I feel.
The breeze caressing my face.
Soaring above this ocean so real,
Salty freedom is all I taste.

Tasting, tasting, this dry victory at hand.
For one more sip, I yearn.
My thirst only quenched by the sea so grand,
A journey to which I now turn.

Turning, turning, to the only way down;
At the bottom, my reward I shall reap.
Attaining success—to quiet the sound—
Forever mine if I just take that leap.

Leaping, leaping, through my mind with such grace
are images of all who I'd leave.
I can't say goodbye—not to one single face:
Silence will bring no reprieve.

A Morning in North Wildwood

A breeze blows cool, soft.
     A velvety touch across my unshaven face,
          carrying the sweet and salty scent of the sea,
A scent only broken by the aroma
     of my morning coffee whispering a sleepy "hello."
          The seagulls join in the welcome of this new day.
A pair of lovers sits atop a wire above the street signs
     at 17th and Atlantic, resting upon the clear blue ocean
sky.
          An airplane passing in the distance leaves behind
A smoky story of another hundred souls.
     Another sip of my coffee reminds me of my good
fortune,
          as the warm taste of possibility lingers on my
     lips.

I Can See Myself

I can see myself in the mirror.
I can see past the horror.
I can see my face clearly.

And it finally
looks like me.

I no longer fear my demons.
I no longer count the reasons.
I forgive myself for past treasons.
I will accept me for me.

And it finally
looks like me.

.

2 DARK

The Color of Nothingness

All alone I sit and stare
at the still silence,
waiting for motion, for color—
for life to emerge—
but the only thing to be revealed
is quiet nothingness.

All alone I sit and stare
counting the hours gone by,
when out of the blue
I see you
bursting with color—
with life—reminiscent
of bygone nights
when we danced,
our ruby lips locked, as if
the yellow night would never
come to an end.

All alone I sit and stare
at your fading shadow,
waltzing along the walls
until there is no color left
but quiet nothingness.

Moonlight's Echoes

Moonlight creeps in
through a nearby window,
Sneaking around the room.
Playing tricks, casting shadows,
    Sleep shall not come soon.

I watch shadowy figures
Dance and sing.
This play—so rousing—
Such joy it brings;
Though, round-and-round,
Tangling
    My mind into jumbled ruin.

The floor, the walls,
You leave no trace.
Shadowy figures
Vanish into space.
The room—empty—
Figures replaced,
By the echoes of moonlight
    standing in place.

Alone

Why do I sit
—alone—
in this empty chair?

Love surrounds me, yet
—alone—
I wallow in despair.

And here I sit, still
—alone—
naked and bare.

Waiting for you
—alone—
to arrive, to repair.

But your eyes
—alone—
the truth they share.

No one will love me,
No one will hold me,
—alone—
No one will care.

Fleeting Seconds

Each passing second
is a moment gone by—
Bringing me closer to "what,"
But further from "why."

Eyes shut tight,
I watch the world pass by:
One fleeting second at a time.

I Sullenly Stare

Black as day;
Bright as night.
Is there even a difference,
when my eyes are shut tight?

No way to know;
No reason to care.
The nothingness I see,
is all that is there.

Nothing on the horizon
but empty despair
Into the void,
I sullenly stare.

Serenity in Silence

the serenity of silence
one only finds in solitude.
so often suppressed
by self-doubt.
unable to summon
the strength
to survive
another step.

No One Will Know

Twinge, flicker, quiver, and curl,
I rile and shake until my dressings unfurl.

On the floor, naked, shrouded in shame,
Alone in this nightmare, huddled in pain.

Invisible to the world around,
Surrounded by people who can't hear a sound.

I scream bloody murder until my lungs explode,
No one takes notice—no one will know.

Close Your Eyes

close your eyes
you're on a train
the pitch is black
your breath constrained

the car is empty
just you and your shame
speeding to nowhere
on these tracks you've lain

enjoy the ride
you've earned this pain
no way out
only yourself to blame

I Desperately Behest

Where do I go?
What do I do?
When did I lose my way?
Why me and not you?

Until I arrive,
My mind won't rest.
Blind will—abandoned.
A single sign,
    I desperately behest.

Alex Hanna

Dust of Ineptitude

So I confidently drive down the empty highway,
speeding to somewhere—not knowing how much gas is in the tank,
not knowing when I'll see the next light of civilization,
only praying I'll get there before I fall asleep at the wheel.

Crashing in the desolate nowhere of my existence
        only means that nobody will find me.
Nobody knows I'm missing.
Maybe they will never look.
But even if they do, I'll be blown away
        like the dust of my own ineptitude.

Long Road Leading Nowhere

On the long road
leading nowhere,
I count the lines
passing me by.

Each a reflection of
years gone by
and a sad reminder
of every goodbye
as I speed towards
the horizon.

What will I find
at the end of the line?
But another long road
leading nowhere.

Miserable Pride

My aching legs—tired, long;
My weary arms—fragile, once strong.

My empty chest—hollow, worn;
My shattered shoulders—bloody, torn;
My naked shame—unworthy, forlorn.

My lonely soul—begging to belong;
My miserable pride—once here, now gone.

Forgotten Reveries

Sadness overshadows
      forgotten reveries.
Light extends no further
      than despondent memories.
But what I find in blindness,
      can never be unseen.

3 FEAR

Fearful Heart

When the lights turn off
and the music stops,
quiet fills the air.
You hear the humming
of silence staring
into the midst
of nowhere.

My heart starts to speak
—leaping beat to beat.
Constricted by fear—
Only muffled words, I hear.

Pumping blood through my veins.
That damn song starts to play.
While no words come through,
I know the tune.

You always seem to find
me when darkness fills my mind.
Alone we shall be:
Forever you and me.

A Moral Injustice

A moral injustice
Presented to me.
Choose to stay?
Choose to flee?

How true is my truth?
How strong is my decree?
I am who I am…
or who you want me to be?

Do I stay in this place,
Pretend to unsee,
The moral injustices
staring at me?

Or do I turn away;
Run from the scene?
My values unbroken,
I blindly live free.

Distant Divide

A distant divide
nears. I must decide
between change and pride.

You live to deride
my every move. You deny
my freedom; forever reside
in my broken mind.

A distant divide
nears. I must decide
between change and pride.

My fate signed
by the hand of my bride,
releasing my broken mind
for me to find
before I arrive
at the distant divide.

Strip Me Bare

strip me bare
to nothing at all
my ego somewhere
but i can't recall

my body now matches
this feeling inside
revealing deep gashes
which will never subside
you see where my hollow
desolation resides

My Depression

I am depressed.
I am not my depression.
My depression is not me.
I am me.
No one defines me
but me.
Especially not my depression.

If I am my depression,
where do I go when
my depression takes pause?
I am still here,
my depression is not.

What if my depression is not depression,
but rather, just *me*?
Then while I am not my depression—
My depression *is* me.

What else am I, then?
What else could I be?
So many things!
Wonderful, exciting, happy things!
But today
I am depressed.
Just depressed.

Brilliance in Sadness

There's a brilliance in sadness
that only few can see.
Most of the world sees black and gray,
But all colors of the spectrum to me.
Viewing the world through a tinted lens,
Such beauty in sadness there be.

I Remorselessly Deprave

I smother
suffocatingly hopeful embers
who will never grow
into the roaring flame
of a misplaced dream—
Dreamt in vain.

I've emptied the air
from their lifeless grave,
breathlessly ignorant,
your innocence,
I remorselessly deprave.

What am I Still Doing Here?

Why am I here?
Looking for what?
It isn't that clear.
They say that the grass
is not always greener.
Then what am I still doing here?

Money, acclaim, love of the chase?
What is it that I seek?
Every option looks dimly bleak.
Sitting here in this foreign place,
I need fresh air—
Just give me some space.
What am I still doing here?

Who Knows Me Better Than Me?

Who knows me better than me?
Who are you to ignore my plea?
Take your presumption, shove it deep inside.
You call yourself a doctor... that title you belie.

Bury your nose back in that chart.
Keep theory and practice far apart.
Behind that veil of ignorance, accountability departs.
Sustenance you refuse to provide.

A Seismic Withdrawal

A seismic withdrawal:
from all that I love;
Isolation I cannot stave.

An eruption of regret:
towers above;
Raining down molten disdain.

Drowning my world:
toxic sludge;
I gasp for what dignity remains.

In hardened rock:
I cannot budge;
In lonely catacombs I am lain.

Unending Night

I open my eyes, you seal them tight.
Staple the lids down, black out the light.
Protect my sleepy eyes from sight.
I'm yours. I'm yours, through the unending night.

The Radio

I turn on the radio
but all I get is static.
Every channel to which I tune
brings more of the same.

The volume steadily increases—
No control over the dial;
And I can't shut it off.

No plug to pull;
No speaker to muffle.
No way to escape
the deafening white noise.

Terminal Unease

A hurried breeze
    blows
Branches on impatient trees
    shake
Swirling leaves round and round
    circle
Shivering street signs until they freeze,
    stuck
        in their post,
        subject to nature's boast,
Swept up by wind's terminal unease.

The Storm Rages

When the storm rages
  before the calm,
How peaceful the sleep
  following a night so long.

But each shocking memory
  of all I've done wrong,
Pounding on my conscience:
  A thunderous song.

Moments

Moments come and moments fade—
Each more fleeting than the last.
"No time like the present."
That's what they said,
But already, the present is past.

4 REGRET

Fade to Black

Deep within, an evil lurks.
It dwells, unnoticed, while Satan smirks.
Carnage, destruction—he leaves in his wake;
Unknowingly hopeful—my soul he will take.

As evil takes over, his power shows clear.
Now consumed by darkness, all I know is fear.
My soul in his mercy, he launches his attack;
No good prevails, just evil—my world fades to black.

His

How do I move forward, when concrete fills my shoes?
My mind is filled with nonsense, my soul is His to use.
As He grabs me and whispers "Hold tight,"
His darkness washes over, blacks out the light;
My will becomes His as I'm consumed by the night,
Forever at His mercy, I have nothing left to lose...

He embraces me gently, knowingly Hell-bound;
Promising His love, while His deviance confounds.
Pain, turmoil, He refused to take—
While comfort, relief, He leaves in His wake.
In reluctant oblige, I am His to make;
We pause, He smirks, and hands me His crown.

Here You Come

Here you come—
I knew you would.
Praying you'd forget,
for once—just once.

Leave me alone.
Leave me be.
I've never done you wrong.

I can't comprehend
why you keep coming back.
You're not welcome here anymore.
No! Nevermore.

I've kicked you out,
changed the locks.
But somehow—
(and I don't know how)
you always return
to haunt me once more.

Why won't you
just leave me alone?
I need to be alone.
Please just leave me alone.

Crisp Sadness

Crisp sadness
    with every bite:
Bright red—the color of my disdain.
Sour desire drips
from the corners
of my indifference.
Hungering for
    the sweet taste of life:
Juicy and tender;
Now rotten,
    but once ripe.

Unready Feet

Enslaved for my past;
Enchained in the present;
Imprisoned for the foreseeable future,
By the perilous plight
Laid at my unsteady,
Unready feet.

Yesterday's Splendid Transgressions

The opacity of the looking glass
dulls the shimmer of the city
with a smoky sheet of sin.

The once-vibrant utopia
reduced to a crumbled memory,
shrouded by the soot of yesterday's
splendid transgressions.

Weary Eyes

I close my weary eyes at last,
Drift into the unknown.
Peering down—despairingly vast—
A tawdry existence we've sewn.

Itchy Bones

My bones itch, marrow burns;
My skin encases unbearable yearns.
I need to escape, need to run wild;
I need to break free from your dastardly guile.

I shake, sweat, and shiver—
I bake in this blizzard.
I find no solace—
Discomfort shimmers

while fire rains down
from snow-covered clouds,
    A perfect contradiction
    in my body's restriction
of feelings that refuse to be bound.
Too tightly riled, I am to be found;
    I pray
    one day
to be unwound.

My Carnivore Mind

Carnivorous thoughts
tear flesh from bone.
Ripping through memories;
no mercy is shown.

The past left in carnage,
a new mind to be sewn.
Fresh blood now soils
the virgin white snow.

Rose Petals Dance

Rose petals dance
across a melodious breeze, fresh
as a budding spring's morn.

Gracefully gliding,
they float with such ease, yet
a melancholy veil they adorn.

The breeze turns violent,
I fall to my knees, rose
petals sting like thorns.

Glancing upward,
towering trees, branches
naked, forlorn.

A breath of wind
whispers my name, exhaling
suffocating scorn.

Clouds overhead
bellow in pain, casting
shame too dense to ignore.

I gasp for a memory—
only nightmares remain, sinking
to my tomb of discord.

Now rose petals fall
as blood-soaked rain, drowning
in this murderous storm.

Tap, Tap, Tap

Tap, tap, tap...
The hollow banging rings out.
Left, right, up, down,
      I can't seem to escape.
Why, why does this tapping persist?
      Solace I shall not take.
Haunting echoes linger about.

Tap, tap, tap, tap...
My mind can find no reprieve.
I scratch and I claw
      until blood drips down;
Why, oh why
      can't I vacate this sound?
In pools of crimson
      I am now surround:
Gasping for air,
      I can't breathe.

Tap, tap, tap, tap, tap...
My God, no more
      can I take.
To end this nightmare
      would bring me such high!
Drowning, sinking,
      in this lonely coffin I reside.
I'd give anything, anything
      if just for a moment—
      the singing and
      ringing subside;
No more options,
      no hope,
I greet the darkness—
      my impending bride.

55

Now the tapping,
     she feeds me my cake.

Tap, Tap, Tap, Tap, Tap, Tap...

Numb

Numb, so numb, I feel nothing at all,
but the frantic beat in my chest.
Plagued by indifference, I begin to scrawl,
Left with this indecipherable mess.

Scratches and gashes all over the walls
blood-curdling screams silence the halls
Fingernail etchings bloody and raw
A sign of my immutable distress.

What I would give to feel anything, anything;
Pleasure—no, pain—would be best.
The sweet release of crimson tears:
My ecstasy, deeper I press.

Imperfect Regret

I crave the sensation of steel through flesh.
>Nothing can feel more true.
Thin chiseled strokes, roses bloom fresh,
>The artist paints with the purest of hues.

The easel, the lighting, my ritual prepared;
I lay out the canvas: naked and bare.
Knifing through fibers, I begin to forget;
On my palette one color, imperfect regret.

The Hidden Truth

I see the truth behind that smile.
You can't fool me with your masterful guile.
The rest of the world may fall for your tricks—
In my eyes, the truth you defile.

Confide in me—it's all for show:
Scrub away that painted-on glow.
It isn't weakness to express how you feel;
To be free is to be real.

I can feel the pain behind your eyes—
a window exposed, let's me into your lies.
"Don't worry," you say, "everything's fine."
I peer in the mirror, and cut another line.

Alex Hanna

Truth

Preaching what you fail to practice—
Just like breathing, you hold your breath,
but only for a passing moment until
the innate, the instinct livens once more.

"Practice makes perfect..." the perfect lie:
A lie so true it becomes truth, itself.
But truth is not truth—only the unyielding
belief that truth is true—
And that's the truth of the matter.

No practice on which you embark will result
in failure, nor success: it will simply
conclude. And that, my dear friend,
is the only truth you can trust.

In Masochism I Bathe

An empty attempt,
Full of contempt.

Burdened with shame;
Only myself to blame.

In this cozy chair, I rock,
Glaring at the clock.

Progress eludes,
I refuse to move.

No, I won't change;
In masochism I bathe.

As I selfishly dwell
in my man-made Hell.

Forever Be Forgot

Write it all down
Seal the letter tight
No return label needed
I won't make it through the night

Slap on the postage
Slip it through the slot
Never be delivered
Forever be forgot

5 HOPE

Where Do I Go?

Where do I go when surrounded by fog
so dense I can hardly breathe?
Repulsively palpable—my lungs filled with smog,
so lost—nobody will grieve.

Impossible to tell
whether it's day or its night.
Fear washes over
that I've seen my last light.
Bruised and bloody—
I'm losing this fight.
Weary legs carry
me further on this plight.
Deeper into madness
until I vanish from sight.

When in my darkest moment,
unexpected delight,
a reassuring voice whispers
"You'll be alright."
Holding me close
in her arms, I'm wrapped tight.
My hope now restored;
she's banished my fright.
We ascend from the fog:
soar to great heights.

How do I convey this feeling so grand?
Ecstasy with each breath I take.
Clarity, levity, I now understand;
Happiness is my will to make.

Liberating Unknown

Lift me up when I'm on my knees.
Nourish my soul with the fruits of your goodness.
Teach me to walk on these once-fettered legs.

Show me the path,
Lend me a torch.
And with a kiss on the cheek,
I boldly step
into the liberating unknown.

Her Radiance Abounds

the cloudy skies begin to yield,
a once-forgotten hope is again revealed,
melting the dew as she kisses the field,
today, her radiance abounds.

This Morning

This morning, the sun rose,
just like every other morning.
But this morning is unlike any
other you have experienced.

This morning marks
a new day,
a new opportunity,
a new you.

And this morning is just
like every other morning—
Only it is the first morning
that you realized this gift.

And every morning after this,
you awaken to a new dawn;
to a sun which beams hope
into your soul.

Make this day special.
There will never be another
like this morning.

Hope

The sunlight shines—
Shines so bright.
After the darkest—
Darkest of nights.
You're tired or fighting—
Fighting this fight.
But tomorrow brings hope—
Hope of new light.

Undying Light

A lighthouse perched upon the shoreline,
     warding off danger in the night.
Her beauty—nothing short of sublime;
     A fire—eternal—shone bright.

Once I've left your safety,
     and you've all but vanished from sight.
Now alone on the open waters,
     my deepest fears take flight.

But on the stormy seas,
     I shut my eyes and pray.
Then off in the distance,
     you pierce through the gray.
Guide me to refuge
     in the calm of your bay.
Through the thickest fog,
my darkest hours,
     you always show me the way.

I am graced forever, by your undying light.

Our Final Night

As our final night comes to pass,
a perilous journey docks at last.

Across stormy seas, the ocean blue,
each harrowing battle strengthened the crew.

On nights we feared the battle was lost,
our brothers dug deeper—no matter the cost.

Standing arm-in-arm, we would proudly stride:
Each man in the crew
quietly knew
we needed each other to survive.

The Mighty Lioness

I wake to stormy seas in the height
of the emptiest night;
> Roaring like a threatened lioness
> protecting her cubs from certain danger.
My brain, scrambled as tomorrow morning's eggs, fails to act
as I sullenly retract,
> a steel sledge hammers the ship,
> snaps the anchor line, which I failed to bring in
> as I mercilessly drift.
Not knowing where you'll take me, I shut my eyes and pray
> that you take me there quicker
> than the lioness kills her prey.
and (if it's not too much to ask) that we arrive by day.

A Place Called Anywhere

I'm on my way
to a place
called anywhere.

Tank full of gas,
getting there fast.

No signs,
no map
to show the way.

Yet still I know
exactly where to go.

Each road to take,
every turn to make.

And when I arrive,
I'll know I'm there—
Finally alive
at a place
called anywhere.

I Live

I live for that moment of hope,
as the sun peaks over the crest
on a cool Spring's morn.

That moment which takes my breath away
like a cool breeze on a warm Summer's day.

The afternoon majesty
of Autumn's brilliant colors—
painting a portrait of God, himself.

The moment of nature's final breath,
as the sun dips below the evening horizon—
to take its Winter's slumber.

For those moments—I live.

Peacefully Silent

Quiet isolation;
Deafeningly alone,
yet peacefully silent.

Fog glides over
the icy clear lake
crafted by millions
of pinpoint perfections:
Exploding in a landscape
of the most vibrant colors:
The bluest of blues,
lilac purples,
sunflower yellows.

Unifying oneness
in nature's
tranquil gifts
bestowed upon all
who stand,
willing to receive,
and to be humbled
by its righteousness.

Slippery Stones

No future, just now;
Not "then," not "when."
Here, now, today, this;
There is no tomorrow's
hopeful bliss.

I hold in my hand
the most precious stone—
what fortune I own!
But I foolishly ignore
and hope for more.

I throw it away
in hopes that one day—
I patiently yearn—
for two to return.

So don't put off today
in hopes of tomorrow;
Don't sacrifice happiness
for certain sorrow.

Bated Breath

Oil burns
just past the stroke
of midnight.

The waning flame
refuses to fade,
as she gracefully dances,
breathlessly glides,
painting her naked portrait
across the flickering stage.

Still for an instant.
A glowing reprieve.
She delicately balances—en pointe—
at the edge of each bated breath.
Suspense captivates,
awaiting the next effortless step.

Dancing Flames

Dance, flicker, move to the beat;
The song is your own,
the music—your feet.
On a sea of possibility,
opportunity—you meet.
On the stage of transcendence
with willing arms you greet.

A Whisper

A whisper so quiet, you can only hear it
when you close your eyes and hold your breath.
A sound so pure—so true—it only exists
in that brief moment between heartbeats—
when the whole world stands still.

With You

Burning light,
in the dead of night,
with my eyes shut tight:
(I still see you.)

Gentle, your figure,
in my dreams, you linger,
the most delicate splinter:
(I still feel you.)

A sensual waft,
subtle—soft,
for a moment I'm lost:
(I still smell you.)

The faintest sound,
yet explosively profound,
your breath surrounds:
(I still hear you.)

Salty sweet,
rolling down your cheek,
to where our lips meet:
(I still taste you.)

Wherever you are,
no matter how far,
the brightest star:
I am still with you.

ABOUT THE AUTHOR

Alex is a full time technologist and all-the-time poet. He uses poetry as a means of self-expression, allowing the words to create the images he ties to emotions.

Alex started writing in 2015. This is Alex's first published work.

www.ingramcontent.com/pod-product-compliance
Lightning Source LLC
Chambersburg PA
CBHW071908020426
42331CB00010B/2715